waterways series

Ventriloquism for Monkeys

releasing new voices, revealing new perspectives

Ventriloquism For Monkeys

waterways
an imprint of flipped eye publishing
www. flippedeye.net

First Edition
Copyright © Niall O'Sullivan, 2007
Cover Image © Niall O'Sullivan, 2007
Cover Design © flipped eye publishing, 2007

ISBN-10: 1-905233-08-6
ISBN-13: 978-1-905233-08-3

British Library Cataloguing in Publication Data
A catalogue record for this book is available from the British Library

Editorial work for this book was supported by the Arts Council of England

Printed and Bound in the United Kingdom

niallosullivanpoetry@yahoo.co.uk
http://niallosullivan.co.uk

Supported by
The National Lottery®
through Arts Council England

Ventriloquism for Monkeys

Niall O'Sullivan
2007

While some like to thank deities or the kindly provisional universe, I can honestly say that I'd be out on my arse if it wasn't for the help of a great many people and organisations, a few of whom are listed below.

Nii Parkes, James Byrne, Tim Wells, Russell Thompson, Geraldine Collinge, Sarah Ellis, Lisa Mead , Angie Bual, Luke Wright, Roddy Lumsden, Paul Lyalls, Nathan Penlington, John Bush, Tom Chivers, Joshua Idehen, Musa Okwonga, Inua Ellams, Fred Voss, Todd Moore, Lucy English, Ely Ahamed, Jessica York, Marijke Brouwer, Martin Jankowski, Jennifer Dautermann, Ailsa Murray, Eirik Bø, Frederik Bjerre Andersen, John Citizen, Ernie Burns, Agnes Meadows, Andy Ching, Graham Buchan, Tony Walsh and all the staff at The Poetry Cafe.

Apples and Snakes, The Poetry Society, The British Council, The Arts Council of England, Creative Partnerships, Shortfuse, Express Excess, Poejazzi, Penned in the Margins, The Wolf, Rising, Write to Ignite, Latitude Festival, Cheltenham Literature Festival, Folkestone Literature Festival, Roskilde Festival, Maya Productions, BAC, thepoem.co.uk

All my love to Mum, Dad, Maricel, Stepdad Paul, Brian, Kim, Ossian, Oliver and Emily.

This book is dedicated to the Phylum Chordata.

Ventriloquism for Monkeys

Contents

Pleistocene

A Once-Famous Ventriloquist Learns to Cope with the Drudgery of a Normal Life

He still scrapes the odd buck
from his most famous creation,
university shows with the odd f-word
to acknowledge his audience have matured.
Halfwit the Hippo and Lord Lovelunch
didn't kick up a storm on e-bay.

His new voices are slightly skewed
variations of the same theme:
a confident chirp for the bank manager,
a geezerish growl down the pub,
and of course, the stage voice
whenever he's recognised at B&Q.

He cleans a few windows to get by,
mostly for *friends of friends,*
catches his weary reflection
as he swipes away the suds,
tries to think of it as another puppet
brilliantly operated by a subtle mind.

Come evening, he dozes
in front of the flicker of his old stage,
the ache of his muscles the symptom
of a new *self* he's building
like the meal ticket he once fashioned
in his father's cluttered shed.

Goodnight my love, he whispers
as he kills the bedside lamp.
Goodnight my darling, I'm so proud of you!
replies the photograph of his ex-wife
pronouncing the *p* in *proud*
with passion and precision.

The Church of Sam

Some say it's easier to die than to live, others the opposite.
I say both are true on different days.
Sam, a local drunk, tried both and failed,
the first with pills, then razorblades…
only to find himself back on the bench,
park bench that is, where he drank with his mates,
broke up their fights, tidied up
after they slunk off to crash in their rooms or the nearest bush.
He showed me his poems, clunky, clumsy rhymers,
unrefined emotion, weary slugs to the gut.
They were like prayers for god to give him the strength.
For what? I never had the balls to ask.

On the day I sprayed the rose beds with poison
he beckoned me over, *Please… don't destroy this,*
pointing out a corner where he'd established his church.
The pews and walls were fashioned from strips of bark
for a congregation of sweet wrappers and orange peel.
He'd reclaimed the word LOVE from an ad in a magazine
and tied it with grass to a lolly-stick cross.
I played no part in its sacking.
Call it the hand of the almighty, or nature's envy;
the hard rain came and knocked it flat
but left the man still standing.

My City

I guess it's somewhere between the twinkle
of Canary Wharf's tip and the last drip
from a sleeping tramp's trouser leg
to trickle down a Soho drain.
Lower still, to the electric trains
that whirr through the dark, the fickle
haircuts of Hoxton, the markets and their tacky crap,
the ghosts of rippers, working girls, the smog.
The river, of course, the river, it's up to you
whether you picture the sunlit glitter
of its surface, or maybe below
for sand, old bones, yesterday's litter.
Tonight's recommendation is my bed.
If not, bollocks, buy an A-Z.

Embedded

After twenty years of hard rain, erosion, gravity's nagging-
the edges of bricks, lumps of concrete and kerbstones
are poking through the grass humps of the BMX track,

giving me pause to remember Blake:
Drive your cart over the bones of the dead
                  or rather
Fly your BMX over the avenues, living rooms and factories of yesteryear,

but, according to the order sent down from the Ranger's office,
this debris has been *embedded* into the grounds
and I have been told to dig it all out.

I find the hypothesis endearing,
the idea that somewhere within this rundown estate
some local crackpot, perhaps an elderly female

with pagan tendencies and supernatural powers,
drags a lump of concrete into this park, and cackling
under the moon's lurid light, stamps it down into the grass.

The image is enough to keep my mind elsewhere as
I wedge my spade under the first lump.
                  If only I too
could get paid 20 grand for my wild and useless narratives.

The Father in Law

He came with the missus, part of the package.
He brought his old chair. His wife's ashes.
He sat there all day, never talking,
not to me or his daughter.
Not to admonish the toddlers
when they threw milk at his trousers.
Not a groan when the dog chewed his toes.
He only opened his mouth to shovel in food
which he chewed slowly, miserably.

He was always the last to leave the living room,
I'd pretend to be interested in Newsnight
hoping he'd go to bed before
they showed those arty films.
Never happened, and when I rose
in the early hours to cut my sandwiches
and head off to the thankless job,
he was there, sat still, scantly lit.
That was when I heard the breathing most;
Innocent particles of oxygen
sucked into the darkest place on earth,
then released, corrupted, polluting the air.
Alone with him, I'd shout
obscenities into his face, did terrible
things to his wife's ashes as he looked on.
Of course, the missus wouldn't put him in a home.
I started thinking that come the day he died,
she'd have him stuffed and sat back on that chair.

The only way that I could get my life back
was if I could make him scream, jump, even twitch.
So I bought a gun from a Polish mate at work,
took it home, stood in front of him, took aim.
Shot the old sod's left ear clean off.
Not a scream, not a jolt, not a bead of sweat
just the smell of hot blood, pouring,
not a tear as I pushed the muzzle into his forehead
not a smile to show that finally, he'd won.

I've heard of men in India that sit
unmoved for years, no food or water,
they do so through some peace they've found within,
but that was never the case with him.
It was some old hatred that kept him going,
something terrible that he would never forgive,
a cold rhythm, fierce quiet where his heart once was.

The Printer, his Wife and the Meme

My life passes quickly while the days go slow,
I do what I must to get by.
I've got three years of marriage that may end soon
and ten hours a day watching the silk screen
spit out the same image a few thousand times.

I read a lot, as the machines slide and whir,
fill my underused mind with things
that make me see the world different.
Today I learnt about the meme, the idea
as a life form, like a virus, biological or digital.

And then it clicked, that the brain
is hardware and ideas are software
and how good ideas and bad ideas rule our lives.
I got so excited by the possibilities
I called up a computer engineer to take a look at my wife.

He arrived bang on time, a skinny twenty-something,
who looked like he saw less sunlight than me.
I led him to the kitchen, where she'd retired
with her mobile to conspire with her friends.
So, where's the computer? - he asked.

I took a while to explain it to both parties
I started off extolling the hardware software theory
and finished by saying we hadn't had sex in six months.
Now within her body, must be a biological urge
caused to malfunction by a virus of the mind…

She started screaming; he tried to leave.
You're not going any where! she snapped
Grabbing the poor boy by his tiny wrist.
Then she calmed down, smiled, whispered *okay*
and led the skinny programmer upstairs.

The process of reprogramming women must be intense,
for I could hear her screaming , moaning,
banging the wall with her palm,
then the boy came down, drenched in sweat
left before I could pay him, silly lad.

Tonight, she cooked my favourite meal,
unplugged the phone and TV.
We drank red wine, chatted for hours
made plans for the future, holidays, children.
When words and bottle ran dry, we went to bed.

After hours of lovemaking with her on top
she nestled her head into my shoulder and whispered
Thank you darling, I'm much better now.
If ever I start to malfunction again
feel free to give that nice young man a call.

The Museum

Last time O'Sullivan walked this far
across the city, spanning three boroughs,
was when the bombs went off. Understand,
it wasn't because he was afraid, he just felt
it made more sense to leave the job and walk
home in the gentle drizzle, keeping his
broken fist, still dressed, under an umbrella.
Halfway back he got a call from his mother.
No-one he knew had died. By the time
he got to Putney he felt better. Not that it mattered.

Today he's walked to a museum, no bad reason,
just that the walls were closing in, his own company
was poison. Right now he's staring hard
at the skull of a Neanderthal, then Homo Erectus,
finally Australopithecus. He's trying to imagine her
eyes, deep within that skull, her skin,
her wild but gentle face. What she would think
of him, unshaven, some warped intelligence
in his greenish brown eyes? He gets a text
from his father who's having trouble
with his medication. He'll be in touch soon
but for now he can't talk to anyone.

O'Sullivan peers again at the ancient skull,
tries to see the case's glass as the millions
of years between now and when that creature breathed,
since she walked out of the forest on two feet.
He wants to reach across the millennia, embrace her,
maybe to let her know how grateful he is
for this walking life she's passed down,
or maybe pin her down to the forest floor
make sure those tentative steps are never taken.

Homo Erectus Catches the Northern Line Home

*"Suitably clothed and with a cap to obscure his low forehead and beetle
brow, he would probably go unnoticed in a crowd today."*
Richard Leakey and Alan Walker *quoted from National Geographic*

*"In his eyes was not the expectant reserve of a stranger but that deadly
unknowing I have seen in a lion's blank yellow eyes."*
Alan Walker, *palaeontologist.*

*"...I would put money on him not having a blank animal stare. We would
have recognised him as a fellow human being."*
Leslie Aiello, *anthropologist.*

It doesn't matter how we got here.
After a day's work, the nagging of tabloids,
on this vicious, mindless urge towards *home*,
our thoughts are far from our origins.

All that matters is that you are *here*,
travelling faster than your species ever dreamed
through dark echoing tunnels, over stern iron bridges,
among this gathering of tiredness and apathy.
With a stolen wallet in your jeans,
a baseball cap disguising your brow ridge,
you've not caused much of a stir among humanity's menagerie.

Your tall, strong body, your stare
that some have conjectured to be similar
to a lion peering blankly from the darkness
has been sufficient in fending off muggers and charity workers.
Yet the glares you have already endured
from well dressed suburbanites, pinstripe gents,
has been enough to teach the survival technique
of staring at the floor.

You are playing this, brilliantly, by ear.
Like the best of us, you have no immediate plans.
Among the lower echelons of this fierce, busy society
a non-committal grunt will get you far.
You may even find a companion, a mate
among this melee of highly strung, flat faced creatures
and tip-toe away into the gene pool's frequencies.

The dying sun flares back at you
from the windows of passing buildings.
The train is coming to a halt,
the doors about to slide open.
You stand as much of a chance as any of us.
One might venture the hard work is already over.
Now remember to swipe your Oyster at the exit barrier.

The Forsaken Shithouse of the Cathode Gods

There's a boozer, south of the river
bares the flaking legend: *real ales, fine wines.*
Not a place for arguments on the use of the comma.
I walk in to a waft of smoke and grungy oak,
huddle round a tiny screen to catch the match.
Tonight, the claret and blues were having a bash
at the world's most public money laundering scam.
Now, understand when I got up from my stool
after Harewood put us one up early on,
it wasn't a display of arrogance;
just that my bladder soaks up lager quicker
than a bumper issue of The Poetry Review.

The gents in that boozer is the place
where all human ideals go to die,
nihilism's Sistine Chapel scrawled in biro.
I picked a cubicle, knowing the seat
would be left up for me as usual.
Pushed the door open only to find
some poor soul, trousers round his ankles
who fixed me with a stare of pure malice,
and as he lifted the BBC mic to his lips
I realised to my horror that it was John Motson.

"...and Reo Coker's given it away to Drogba!
He's looking for Lampard who's on his own...
Hislop's coming off the goal line and it's in!
Lampard has equalised against his old team!"

Within seconds I was back in the bar
smoking my first fag in three years

watching the blues in a celebratory huddle
then the replay of Lampard nutmegging Hislop,
and every syllable of Motson's excitations
was crack-laced mercury pulsing my stomach and spine.
I drank and smoked, ignoring my bladder
watched the match til the end, not caring who won
then eyeballed the door to the gents,
waking with a shriek to the bell of last orders.

So was it a dream?
There was only one way to find out.
I stormed back into the gents
opened the door with a firm shove
and sat there, trousers round ankles,
microphone to his thin leering lips
was not John Motson, but Michael Burke.

"Good Evening, a grisly discovery
in South London, Niall O'Sullivan
little known poet and literature promoter
was found...
                 and I ran, out of the boozer
and into the biting winter cold, shadows
of lamp lit skeletal branches spindling
across my face, the moon and the unblinking
red tip of the Crystal Palace transmitter
leering over my shoulder...

Earthquake

No-one was killed in the great London earthquake,
well, not by falling phone masts or vanishing
through sudden fissures in the road,

though there were heart attacks,
suicides not wanting to be cheated of their choice.
One guy was mauled by his own shit-scared Dalmatian.

I was in the centre of town,
stuck in a daydream, as others
ran for shelters that would collapse any moment.

The homeless laughed from their reserved doorways.
Rats ran up the subway stairs
as shrieking commuters ran down.

The gables of parliament bent sideward
in a rare moment of honesty.
Terrorists went back to the drawing board.

I overcame a lifetime of Catholic shyness,
wondering if I was still dreaming
as I pushed up a stranger's skirt,

ripped her panties off in a fit
of clumsiness rather than passion,
miscuing her a dozen times

before I sank right in.
She screamed, dug her nails into my thigh
then shouted *Yes Gordon, yes!*

Husband's name, I thought,
followed by *Christ, do I look like a Gordon?*
as the millennium wheel rolled into the Thames.

Within a week the TV signals were running again,
so the experts could tell us
that the earthquake never happened.

Impossible, no plates beneath us
to shift in the first place. Some argued
until the last lick of paint dried,

then it was only the shouting
of conspiracy nuts in musty poetry holes,
that no-one gave a fuck about.

I breezed through the years
like a plastic bag down a high street,
until I saw her again,

classy, glacial, out of my league,
a woman and her family leaving
the Tate gallery,

and, apart from the expensive clothes,
Gordon and his two year old son
looked just like me.

Prayer Candles

More than the enamelled icons,
the stern gables, stations of the cross,
the candles lent a sense of something alive
as we stood knelt, sung, prayed, daydreamed,
stifled in our ridged Sunday best,
they mirrored and mocked us,
the congregation of our needs and supplications,
shivering and naked.

I never made the rank of alter boy,
never had to pace the empty church,
mercilessly snuff them one by one.

Tonight, in my room,
I've never felt as far
from the beggar's grasp,
the wars are safely shut behind the TV screen,
but as we light the candles,
let's remember them anyway,
though those little flames will barely live
as long the seed I have spilt
in all dubious manner of person and place
in the eighteen years it's been
since my last confession,

I can choose none better than you
to take those short steps to the desk
push your hair to one side
and extinguish my prayers
with a gentle drawn out breath.

Barcelona

Last week, in England, I asked you
whether the soul of an elephant was bigger
than the soul of a cabbage white butterfly.
You said all souls are immeasurable.
Yesterday, we navigated the narrow crags
between the chiselled brown bodies
rolled across the beach like some cross
between Baywatch and Dunkirk.

We walked, fuelled by the stubbornness
in refusing to admit
the utter disappointment
of being on holiday.
I envied a madwoman laid down
on the Barceloneta pavement, smiling
at the shapes the palm trees made, a cigarette
long dead between her fingers.

It was the plate of mussels that saved us,
the largest we'd seen, the fresh killed creatures
between the quartz black shells were floppy, lippy
and more than a little bit cunty,
drowned in the hot fatty juice of a fatal orgasm.
We swallowed them whole and tasted
a forgotten salt immensity, our stomachs pulsed
as their souls billowed out, immeasurable, within our own.

Dear Chris

I remember you from my college days,
huge silver headphones clamped around your neck.
While my sketchbooks were crammed with pseudo-cubism,
yours were full of tag designs
and dynamically posed anatomical impossibilities,
a kind of ghetto twist on the Jack Kirby style.

On the night we set out to the brave new world of pub
the doorman wouldn't let you in because
you wouldn't fasten your trousers above your waist.
It was a bizarre stand off, his nonchalance, dwarfing you,
your incandescent rage, perhaps because he was a brother too.

Last place I saw you was at the hospital,
a bright spring day, the only traffic-
wild geese waddling across empty roads.
I could hear the river, breeze through long grass.

I was visiting my dad,
apart from the odd bout of the shakes, chain smoking,
I could tell he had his exit strategy planned,
he'd been in far worse scrapes than this. But Chris,
you were there too, somnambulant,
slippered, smiling softly.

Your hair was an unkempt afro
that has since become trendy.
Although those headphones
weren't clamped round your head,
I couldn't stop thinking of them.
You whispered something I couldn't quite make out.
Your trousers were fixed above your waist.
You weren't angry anymore.

From My Window

I'm a better man when I'm not thinking of others.
A washing line sways emptily with the breeze.
Tower blocks, houses, windows, bricks, endless,
Not a single human in view, just the evidence.

A washing line sways emptily with the breeze.
The trees are ready to burst, it won't be long now.
Not a single human in view, just the evidence
The coriander pot on the sill is doing well.

The trees are ready to burst, it won't be long now,
For now, the branches are decked with a foliage of crows.
The coriander pot on the sill is doing well
A rhythm, a rhyme scale of cells repeating themselves.

For now, the branches are decked with a foliage of crows
If I screamed out loud would it change anything that I see?
A rhythm, a rhyme scale of cells repeating themselves.
The horizon flames red with pollution, I take a deep breath.

If I screamed out loud would it change anything that I see?
Satellite dishes tilt upwards, conversing with space.
The horizon flames red with pollution, I take a deep breath.
With my hand to the pane, my palm soaks up light like a leaf.

Satellite dishes tilt upwards, conversing with space.
Tower blocks, houses, windows, bricks, endless.
With my hand to the pane, my palm soaks up light like a leaf.
I'm a better man when I'm not thinking of others.

The Book of My Life

Who would've thought that I'd find the damn thing
on a grotty Finsbury Park pavement.
A natty paperback, flapping about,
god only knows who left it there.

It was the book of my entire life,
every detail was present in the early chapters;
the lies I told during my first confession
my virginity lost on the local cricket square.

I skipped to the final pages -darkened room,
shortness of breath, tears, forced laughter,
prayers mumbling like flies trapped behind glass.
Quite a dull affair, come to think of it.

Trouble came, of course, when I found the present.
How odd, I thought, as I read of how odd I thought it was,
not knowing whether the spatters on the pages
were real raindrops, or the ones I read about.

Right now, I'm in the middle of a long train journey.
The fields are a holy blaze of snow.
But how do I know that I'm not still reading the book,
causing a scene, catatonic on the pavement?

I know, if that was true, I'd be reading about reading,
this train journey wouldn't happen, imagined or not.
But maybe that book wasn't really a book,
but a demon in disguise?

I glimpse a red kite hovering over fields,
wires pass overhead like they were strung up this morning,
some local idiot waves to me from his garden.
This fresh world, my full life. *How perfect.*

The Myth of the Full Circle

Maybe it was because of love
that you never asked what he was thinking
as he sat, stock still yet adrift, tossed
forward and back from *then* to *there*
to *what could be* before the pang of *was*.
He never knew the fireside's warmth unless
some other part of him was swallowing
cold sea-water, his father barking
at him to *swim damn it swim!*

You knew
that sometimes, when he glanced across
the tundra of a pillow into your eyes,
he was staring beyond you into the still-warm
embrace of the women that came before you
each one opening to become the next
and beyond that, the peace he still couldn't grasp
as arms and legs and kisses clamped around him.

He was blustered, tossed in the foam of every
memory that still had nails to snag him;
an unpaid bill, suddenly remembered
when the whisky and the candle's glow
had almost softened his passage into evening.

He was all things at all times in his life, until
his eyesight dimmed, his hefty swagger slowed,
his breath slunk into the hovel of his lung
and memories, the old triumphs that had
been his relief and his torture, yes, they also
stepped slowly backwards into the shadows,
before this fierce machine, this tall proud I
stopped chugging, stopped completely,
became the nothing it was before it *was*.

All that was left did not go into the ground;
You took the idea of *him* back home,
you put on the kettle, tea for one
plus every touch that made you who you were.
He rises every now and then in your own loop
of rerun pleasures and regret, in the same way
that after a star dies, its light travels on
weakening with every aeon passed
until it reaches the end of everything.

holocene

parklife - late august

two days after the storm
the trees of acton park
are creaking
in a breezeless heat
a creaking you could only discern
by digging your fingernails
into the ground

the beautiful need blankets
between their bronzed skins and the grass
laid down on a slow sweat
a sexual inertia
you soon bore of watching

the real stories
always sit on the benches
a 41 year old virgin squints
through booming specs into a bible
while nibbling crustless squares
of honey sandwiches

two benches from there
is the catch of the day
a traffic warden
she's been sat for two hours
legs crossed in the same position

she was out in it
two days ago
drenched to the bone
a fair run from shelter
when lightning struck
the tree above her

never had she felt as scared
and yet
she felt she had been chosen
for what?

she still hasn't figured it out
chain-smoking mayfairs
patches of sweat
forming on her uniform
the ticket book not yet opened
as slowly
a cumulous of heartaches
regroup within her

shallow man

he's realized that you stop looking to the future
when it's shrunk to the size of the crumb
all that's left is to gawp at the past
its every jagged ripple like a frozen ocean

in years gone by his fists have done the banter
he still wears that reputation
like the fluorescent jacket that flaps about
as he bowls into the yard with a sick joke on his lips

sometimes in the evening   before heading down the local
he breaks down in tears in front of his wife
over trivialities like the lotto numbers   wipes his face
in disgust   like it was another man's arse

if he wolf whistles   shouts you down in the street
winks at you strangely   pay him no mind
he makes it his business to show you the shallows
for he fears someone will drown in his depths

buddleia

many faced and silent
the orient has dawned upon the city
the breeze is thick with seed
life digs into dirt
prods into grime
finds a way

do not assume
that this lone branch
sprung from brick
feels loneliness
not with its progeny
sentried along railways
their purple flames emerging
from redundant chimneys

we can howl
and shout
from smashed out windows
as loud
and drunk as we like

our words will never mint the dark
or say so precisely
what we so simply are
to places
people
we will never know

time keeping

of course it isn't real
a bore to the eye
of some awesome mind
it's just echoes and waves
transient
like the thumb scrawled gags
of teenagers
on white vans

I am late for work
after watching
the lifespan
of a rainbow
over southfields park
mid-autumn
a night's leaves
have fallen
waiting for ian
and his tractor
to hoover them up
leaving ruts and tyre tracks
soon to vanish too

in five minutes time
I'll get a bollocking
from my supervisor
I'll consider his new grey hairs
and the way his dulcet yap
gets lost
in the west london soundscape

if he demands a reason
I will show him this poem
my scrappy penmanship
stillborn phrases
fossilised in scribble
this constant failed attempt
at keeping time

denmark

tabloid hypnosis on rush hour trains
miserable fluorescent jackets in oil-slicked yards
the sandy grids of soil between actons paving slabs
then back on that train   too beat to read the daily star

not today

today I'm topless and cross-legged
facing the calm slivers of the baltic sea
the foam is neclaced with baby jellyfish
too weak to defy the gentlest of tides

the blue sky doesn't keep the clouds from passing

that's the line I plunge into again
and again into the trance   into my own blue
my colleague interrupts, whispers – *niall! behind you!*
– a juvenile bull scraping his hoof across the ground

fuck off outta my field buddha boy

it takes a while for the subtle message to sink in
but I up and leave the pimp to his *bidness*
I pass on back to my own rivulet of life
knowing full well I'm the little cloud round these parts

dycentra – bleeding heart plant

it's not your fault
that your flowers are the colour
and shape of romantic hearts
which split from the bottom
emitting an immaculate white droplet

while others are moved
to cluck and coo
like rabid aunties
I've always thought of you
as the chris de burg
of the plant world

never mind

may your seeds be sifted
into sachets
to be given away with copies
of the mail on sunday

my notion of heartache
will always be this

a bramble snaking
through a dark alleyway
with only thorns to bare
having given its fruits
too freely

on never knowing you in the dark

you smile and close the door
accept the delayed embrace
of your understandably impatient lover

along the plane lined street each lamp
sketches its version of my shadow
onto the pavement   cracked by thirsty roots

perhaps there is still a trace of me
a swirl of electrons   a clacking of ions
to suggest I am still inside

the living rooms acoustics still trembling
with my laughter   the heat of my lips
humming along the rim of an espresso cup

perhaps your bedroom light has already gone out
as across the street a car starts
headlights falling across a blossoming rose

which glows as if the electricity was its own
a sketch of light that vanishes forever
as the car pulls away

hard is the journey

– after li po

smudged glasses of warm stella
three pounds a pint
damp pitas of pungent meat
costing another fiver

I throw my kebab down
stamp it into the ground
raise my fists and stare
wildly about me

black cabs will not cross
this many bridged river
it's at least another hour before
I can climb the night bus's steps

crossing the bridge
I toss my change over the side
imagine the warm sun
rising over my shoulder

hard is the journey
hard is the journey
so many false short cuts
– bollocks, where am I?

as the change breaks
the waters calm   I sing
a drunk song to the clouds
– sail across the oceans!

wildlife documentary

sometimes my dark thoughts come
when I'm waiting for a train
must be the empty tracks
rolling in and out of sight
no need to discern
beginning from end
just remember
neither run forever

a fox is staring at me
from the other side
of the chain link fence
I am a poor distraction
a lonely ape in a fleapit zoo
go on   do something
he seems to say
jump like that tosser did last week

I am happy for his company
happier to see him here
than in some forest
as he turns
catches a passing rat
between his teeth
and vanishes
into a tumble of greenery

he remains in my head
as the train pulls in
a blur   a synaptic flash
between graffiti and blackberry
neon and brick
a fierce redness framed
within our dying world

local fame

at fifteen I was the lousiest
car thief in slough
if you ever found your motor
crashed into a tree
metres
from where you parked it
the night before
                    sorry

now a thirty something
mild as the hint of spring
beyond my study window
mild as the first sip of wine
at this desk
tapping away

there is still something
that slips from my grip
sends me plunging
into a darkness
from which
I may never return

after the beating

you've been out on the tiles for weeks
sucking smoke through plastic bongs in the park
putting bricks through car windows
getting served at the bar in your older clothes

but now the pendulum has swung the other way
you've limped home   trembling fingers
making a fudge of getting in quiet
you hear the telly in the living room

you know you can't hide this one
so you announce you presence
not even had time for a spray of lynx
or a gobful of extra strong mints

you step in   mum gasps
at the cuts bruises swellings
on her baby's face   dad gasps too

your immaculate unmarked knuckles

plato buddha and the twitching pricks of pie starved academics

I mentioned how I used to meditate
and he flew into a rage
kicking at my legs while shouting
– *you're not enlightened! you're not enlightened!*

and yet   perhaps I was
because I didn't punch his fucking lights out
he was a skinny student in a stupid hat
he kicked like mr burns

it was late   there had been drinking
debate on the big issues
and of course
females were in attendance

enlightened?   no
just older   wiser to the facts
that late rising's sated my nerves
warm sex dampened my wrath

now hear this
all you learned men
who harp on about buddha and plato
through wine-stained lips at 1am bars

if george bush had tits
and blow job lips
you'd be digging your boners into his thigh
while singing the sad ballad
                          of your lives

twilight

milks the air of brixton town
shadows with a dozen grasping hands
creep out the alleyways

its blue tints the windows of hampstead
letting the trophy wife know
it's okay to pour the first glass

for a second the city boy
hits a rush of nostalgia
his washboard stomach college days

an old song glints in this rare light
survives the busker's attempt
at killing it forever

in a shadowed soho alley
that slumped form could be a vagrant
or a tourist in desperate need of medical help

as above ravens and doves
fold into their branches   tiny hearts
ticking in sync with the markets

and I fall into you
exhausted   no words   no fight left in me
catch me darling if you can

for everything in this hour
has become liquid   dragged in tides
towards a dawning moon

the morning show

funny
our need for this auditorium
our need for film   holding hands
cooling from last night's heat

three weeks
the shock and excitement
of each others bodies
scent of your skin
on my bed linen

last night
you dreamt of an alligator
that guarded my bedroom
from peepers and knockers
I dreamt of a cash machine
dispensing condoms
and hot chocolate

leaves wilt outside
the wind's wet fist knocks a path
through daydreams   clearance
for october's first frost
ignore it all   just an interlude between two
dreams within the dark

the speakers crunch to life
the first reel spins in front of the glaring bulb
I squeeze your palm again
the dream begins

o'sullivan's lost it

where once he dug holes in the sunshine
cared for roses in cut throat estates
he now gloats at home drinking stubbies
only confides with dead men

he says cruel things to the poets
doesn't treat them as the sensitive
creatures they are   like the daisies
he once wrenched from concrete

bang to blog rights
grassed up by google
he knocks back another leffe
and the advances of litty nymphets

as the poets put the world to rights
in smoky after hour bars
he's catching the 68   swearing
at strangers   exhausted

back home   head spinning
he tries hard not to wake his beloved
in the dark kitchen he smells chicken
still warm in the pot   and smiles

a lifetime's ambition

they never saw it
not through my hard studies
the straight-a path I cut
to this career

I opened the only academy
devoted exclusively
to the highest science
the neurology of relativity precognition

I smiled for the cameras
accepted the accolades
dumped the awards when I got home
drunk and pawing some starlets starfish

only when hawking
pledged his grey matter
to my cause
did they confer discreetly
nod their solemn heads
one by one and agree
to open the vault
present me with my prize

– bring him back
let's see
what the shortness
of his life denied the world

I accepted the task
drove home elated
the greatest mind of our time
on the passenger seat

the fools
it was already too late

when the swat team busted through
my kitchen door
I swished the last morsel
through the rich
garlic and red wine sauce
raised my champagne glass
triumphant
as the first bullet cracked my skull

ascension (1)

a middle aged man lies still
  on the patchwork pavement
his skin a mottled brown
  his clothes expensive and ironed
by someone that loves him
  though the ambulance is punctual
the driver shrugs   prompting discreet whispers
  into longwave radios   within minutes
we hear the hum   vicious blades
  a red helicopter descends
a crowd has gathered   pointing
  cameras   video phones   recording all
we no longer trust our eyes
  the man is strapped down tight
loaded onto the chopper
  the blades quicken again
our hands ascending with it
  some of us applauding
as the bronzed well dressed man
  is lifted into the clear blue sky
beyond the grubby buildings
  beyond our grubby lives
forever

claim to fame

at the turn of the last century
my mate's great grandfather became
the first man in scotland to die
beneath the wheel of a steam roller

the only given reason
– *because he was drunk*
raises more questions
than answers

first thoughts
must fall on the driver
perhaps he panicked
confused gears and levers

maybe he maintained his grip
kept his chin up as ribs crunched
as innards shot up through the mouth
like toothpaste through a tube

I think of the victim
whether his last words
were along the lines of
come on then

perhaps he caught a whiff
the stubble of forests
weeping ice caps
the fury of the severed atom

took it upon himself
to pit tendon and bone
against that terrible bloody wheel
before it could gather pace

the sydenham panther

– after rilke

these are the only bars you know
the codes your artefacts wore
before you owned them
the pine picketing of your suburban garden

that a sinewed
rage of black flashed through
knocking you down with the violence
of opening buds and vanishing

leaving a twinge of reality
hard wired to your spine
blood drying onto your cheek
the moment already dead

ascension (2)

no it's not a flying tiger
but a helium filled likeness
escaped from a chubby infant's paw
whose tears hit the ground as the tiger   rises

the beatification of jimmy the grass

big vince   always one for tradition
night night Jim   time to kip with the kippers
a last stock take of street lamps and traffic
and with a heavy heave they tipped me over

a whoosh   the last I knew of air
all shrill in my ears
and then the plonk and clop
a filthy cold   the thickest dark

muddy murk   but which?
the murk of the canal
or the murk of my life
the smutty tape rewinding?

snug in my concrete loafers
I knew better than to struggle
I let the water into my lungs
allowed the silt to settle

behold!   my moonlit kingdom
trolleys   bike frames   beercans
patrolled by pike and perch
my place within it   immortal

bt tower in low cloud

without

no longer the tallest in the city
it's trying to vanish with dignity
to fade into white   like a hackneyed
dream sequence   like scott's corpse *(captain)*

to take its place in an immortal
architectural pantheon
reflected in the crystal palace's glass
smirked at from between the colossus's legs

within

mr big paces his office
-in the midst of this strange whiteness
pulsing in from the windows
it's hard to believe
in the lower floors
the stained pavement
the horizon

last night he watched *crouching tiger*
and sobbed into his merlot
he muses on casting himself
out of the window
to be borne from that cloud

into a happier outcome
maybe that journeyman jazz dude
he once saw at scott's *(ronnie)*
or a happy chimney sweep
dancing across blue tinted rooftops
dancing despite his soot filled shoes
his dodgy accent
that red hot cock tease
and her magic umbrella

empty cinema

take a seat   without popcorn or cola
  houselights up   auditorium empty
the movie doesn't start for twenty minutes
  you watch the blank white screen   enthralled
it only looks like this twenty minutes a day
  sometimes it's a black screen   the same
as the doors and walls when the lights are off
  no   maybe it's a slight glowering rectangle
barely existing thanks to the scant green glow
  of the emergency exit signs
                                        otherwise
it's adventures   twenty four frames per second
  everyone stares   not knowing
what it really is   in the same way
  they stare at all things – *apples   windows   genitals*

ultimately   a blank white screen
  is the hardest damn thing in the world to look at
try it   within seconds your head is throbbing
  with all those water torture pop songs
images of all those old loves that did or didn't
  things you'd say to the boss if you had a pair

it takes another ten minutes to accept
  white screen   framed in black   silence   inhale   exhale
it's funny   you paid to get in here for noise
  CGI   spectacle   explosions   heroes   heroines
only to find you needed the exact opposite

at which point you're rabbit punched
  by the *pearl and dean* jingle   within seconds
a piss weak american beer becomes your sole passion
  enslaves your tongue to your eye

NOTES

A Once Famous Ventriloquist Learns to Cope with the Drudgery of a Normal Life
- Loosely based on the following Zen koan:

The Monk Zuigan used to start every day by saying to himself out loud: "Master, are you there?"
And he would answer himself, "Yes sir, I am!"
Then he would say, "Better sober up!"
Again he would answer, "Yes sir! I'll do that!"
Then he would say, "Look out now; don't let them fool you!"
And he would answer, "Oh no, sir, I won't! I won't!"

The Printer His Wife and the Meme
- This poem is more a parody of the "greedy reductionist" rather than a swipe at the fascinating proto-science of Memetics. See the final chapter of Dawkins' The Selfish Gene and Susan Blackmore's The Meme Machine for more.

Homo Erectus Catches the Northern Line Home
- The poem and the quotes that precede it refer to Nariokotome Boy or Turkana Boy (KNM-WT 15000), a 1.5 million year old Pleistocene hominid found in Kenya in 1984. Some palaeontologists refer to his species as Homo Ergaster, and save the name Erectus for later descendents that spread out as far as East Asia.

a lifetime's ambition
- Based on a hazy recollection of a documentary about Einstein's brain. Kept in slices in a formaldehyde jar, it reminded me a bit of pickled calamari.

the sydenham panther
- In March 2005 Tony Holder, a former soldier, saw his pet cat cornered by another animal in the bushes at the bottom of his garden in Sydenham, south London. He went to the rescue only to be pounced on by an animal about 4ft long. "It sent me sprawling on my back in the bushes. Its huge teeth and the whites of its eyes were inches from my face," he said. "I was fighting for my life. I was grappling with it for a good two minutes before it ran off." Holder was left with a large scratch on his face, a bitten finger and a cut wrist.

The Church of Sam, Embedded, parklife - late august, shallow man, time keeping and denmark
are all based on day to day experiences from when I worked as a gardener for Acton Council.